When I Was Eight

David Bouchard
Art by Laszlo Veres

Literacy Consultants
David Booth • Kathleen Corrigan

When I was eight, Kokum
took me into the forest.

"Boy," she said.
"It is time you come to know
who you are.
You need to know who you are."

My grandmother loved to talk,
and I loved to listen.

"Creator has given you many gifts,"
said Kokum.
"But one of your gifts is special.
It is for you to discover.
You need to live your life
using that gift."

"But how will I find my gift, Kokum?"
I asked.

"There is no better way to learn
than by learning from those around you.
Come, let's walk," said Kokum.

I remembered the smell of the bannock
Kokum had packed early this morning.
I knew this would be a good day.

"Look at Beaver over there."
Kokum was pointing toward the river.
"What do you see?"

"I see Beaver working hard," I replied.
"The lodge seems to be built,
but Beaver is still working!"

"Do you work as hard as Beaver, boy?"

"No, Kokum, I do not," I replied.

We walked farther into the forest.
We stopped at a clearing.
Kokum stared at a small black dot
off in the distance.

"Can you see Bear, my grandson?"
asked Kokum.
"What do you know of Bear?"

"I am not sure, Kokum," I answered.
"Well, I guess Bear is strong.
Bear is … very courageous?"

"And you, my grandson?
Do you have the courage of Bear?"

"No, I do not think so, Kokum.
But I think you do," I replied.

"And there …"
Kokum was looking off toward
Grandfather Sun.
"Can you see them?"

I looked closely. It was a wolf pack!
They were moving toward the lake.
I heard them almost every night,
but I did not see them very often.

"They are beautiful, Kokum," I said.

"Yes, but what do you know of Wolf?"

"I know that the pack is very important to Wolf, Kokum," I answered.
"I know the pack respects the leader.
The pack is humble.
Wolf is humble and respectful."

"And you, boy?" asked Kokum.
"Are you like Wolf?"

I laughed out loud.
"No, Kokum, I am a little shy,
but I do not think I am humble."

We spent the day
walking through the forest.
Kokum pointed out all of the animals,
from Buffalo to Ladybug.
Kokum let me think about what each
animal had and what animal I might be.

I remember looking toward the trees when she spoke of Owl's great vision.
Then we saw Eagle sitting proudly from on high.
We then watched Turtle, sitting on a dry patch of dirt next to the lake.

"No, Kokum, I am not Eagle," I said.
"Eagle is very important.
I am not as important.
Eagle can talk with Creator.
I have much to learn from Turtle too.
I think I waste too much.
I have to put back what I do not use just as Turtle teaches us."

Kokum started to say less and less.
I found myself leading her teaching.
I soon saw tiny animals and bugs.
I knew that each animal had something
special, and so did I.

"Kokum, I see myself
in so many of these animals,
but none are quite like me," I said.

I turned to look at my grandmother.
Kokum was sitting on a tree stump.
In her hand was a piece of bannock,
and pulling on it was Raven.

Raven was courageous and respectful.
Raven worked hard.
Raven was a little bit of everything,
and I was too. I was like Raven!

I was eight when I learned who I was.
I thought Kokum was my teacher,
but now I know better.

We learn from our family,
our friends, and our neighbors.
We are all one family,
and everyone teaches us.